a popactivism book

CAN YOUR
SMARTPHONE
CHANGE THE
WORLD?

Erinne Paisley

ORCA BOOK PUBLISHERS

Cataloguing in Publication information available from Library and Archives Canada

Issued in print and electronic formats.
ISBN 978-1-4598-1303-8 (softcover).—ISBN 978-1-4598-1304-5 (pdf).—
ISBN 978-1-4598-1305-2 (epub)

First published in the United States, 2017
Library of Congress Control Number: 2017932496

Summary: This work of nonfiction, in the PopActivism series for teens, looks at how you can use a smartphone as a tool for social justice.

Orca Book Publishers is dedicated to preserving the environment and has printed this book on Forest Stewardship Council® certified paper.

Orca Book Publishers gratefully acknowledges the support for its publishing programs provided by the following agencies: the Government of Canada through the Canada Book Fund and the Canada Council for the Arts, and the Province of British Columbia through the BC Arts Council and the Book Publishing Tax Credit.

Edited by Sarah N. Harvey
Design by Jenn Playford
Front cover and flap images by Ute Muller
Back cover images by Getty Images, Heather Nichols, Erinne Paisley
Author photo by Jacklyn Atlas

ORCA BOOK PUBLISHERS
www.orcabook.com

Printed and bound in China.

20 19 18 17 • 4 3 2 1

To my parents

CONTENTS

ACTIVISM

The creation of social and/or
political change.

POPACTIVISM

Activism fused with pop culture.

popactivism
see change, share change, be change

"What is interesting is the power and the impact of social media...So we must try to use social media in a good way."

—*Malala Yousafzai*

1

THE GIRL IN THE PAPER DRESS

IN MAY OF 2015, my brother took a few pictures of me and my friends at our senior prom. There were the usual group pictures, the candid laughing shots and, of course, the artistic snaps of corsages. My graduation weekend was filled with hugs, tears, reflections on the last four years of high school, and daydreams of future plans. People always say high school goes by quickly, but you never quite realize how true that is until you're up on stage, reaching for your diploma and having a mini panic attack about what's coming next. Throw in a celebration involving as many friends and family members as possible, and you get one intense weekend. On Monday morning I was happy to wake up to memories of the weekend—and a whole slew of photos posted for the world to see online.

I've always loved the thrill of the little notification that pops up on your screen when you get "tagged" or someone "likes" or comments on a photo. Maybe it's the anticipation mixed with a bit of fear. You never know what could be waiting on the other side—an unflattering mid-speech photo, a cute group shot. There's a leap of faith involved in allowing your life to be displayed online. The notifications came in a few at a time, but in the hours and days that followed, these notifications quickly ballooned from one or two,

SOMETHING EXTRAORDINARY WAS HAPPENING: MY STORY WAS GOING VIRAL.

Graduation day! My best friend had to keep tape in her purse just in case fixes were needed! STUART PAISLEY

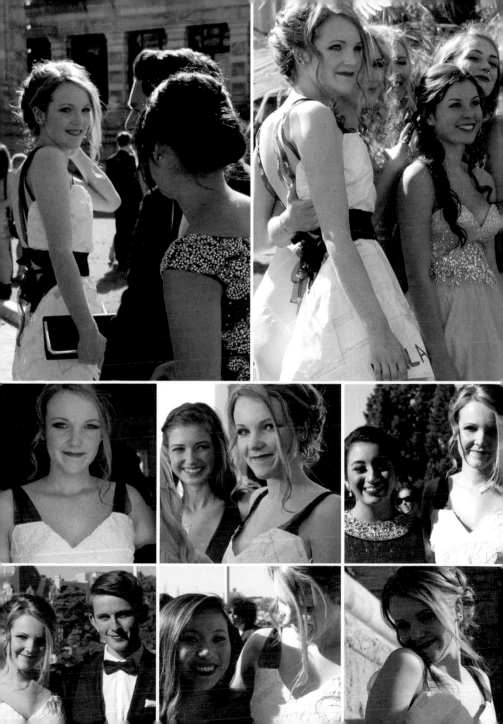

I've recieved my
Not every woman

AALA.ORG

With my friend Amadea
Gareau on the steps of
the British Columbia
Parliament Buildings.
STUART PAISLEY

to one or two hundred, to one or two thousand. Something extraordinary was happening: my story was going viral.

PAPER, TAPE AND A RED PEN

So what happened on my graduation weekend that made me "trend in style" on MTV.com above Kim Kardashian, Willow Smith and Rihanna? I wasn't wearing the most cutting-edge, high-fashion Louis Vuitton dress. In fact, I was wearing a dress that cost me zero dollars and was made in my living room. I built my prom dress out of old math homework, Scotch tape and a bit of black satin. With a red felt-tip pen (the same kind teachers use to mark tests) I wrote *I've received my education. Not every woman has that right. Malala.org.* Then I donated the money I would have spent on a prom dress to the Malala Fund.

In my hometown of Victoria, British Columbia, the story took off like wildfire. I was getting photo requests from local newspapers, and radio stations were calling to interview the "girl in the paper dress."

I was ready to talk about my creation, but that's not all I wanted to talk about. I knew people would be listening, and I wanted them to know that my reason for making the dress was not just because it looked cool.

More than 130 million girls in the world are out of school. Let's make it zero. This is the first sentence you see when clicking on malala.org. This is the fact that inspired me to make the dress. Malala Yousafzai was born in 1997, the same year as me, in the Swat Valley, Pakistan. She has an immense passion for learning, and she believed in everyone's right to an education. In 2009 the Taliban's military presence in the Swat Valley created fear about girls going to school, and Malala spoke out about it. In an anonymous blog she wrote for the BBC, Malala talked about her fears of a military attack on her school, the bans on music and television, the restrictions being placed on women, and many other realities she was facing. As her voice grew stronger and her story became more and more well known, the Taliban decided to silence her.

In 2011 they pledged to murder her. On October 9, 2012, Malala was shot on a school bus on her way

Malala Yousafzai is the same age as I am. If we had been born in the same place, we could have been in the same school classroom.
JSTONE /SHUTTERSTOCK.COM

Women who receive an education are much less likely to be victims of child marriage and more likely to give back to their communities. TRAVEL STOCK/SHUTTERSTOCK.COM

to class. She survived and was flown to the United Kingdom for intensive care. In the weeks after the attack, over two million people signed a right-to-education *petition*, and the National Assembly of Pakistan swiftly ratified Pakistan's first Right to Free and Compulsory Education Bill. Malala's story was the top news worldwide, and since then her voice has only continued to grow stronger and stronger. She founded the Malala Fund, wrote the bestselling book *I Am Malala*, starred and wrote for the documentary *He Named Me Malala*, and even received the Nobel Peace Prize.

EDUCATION IS A RIGHT

I made my paper dress because millions of girls around the world have had their right to an education taken away from them, and I had taken this right for granted. The only difference between those girls and me is that I was born in Canada.

In many ways, prom is a time to celebrate high school achievements and anticipate newly available opportunities such as further education, work or travel. When I thought about this, it made sense to use the money and attention that goes into grad to improve educational opportunities for those who are denied that right. The Malala Fund works to provide twelve years of free education for every girl in the world. It has built a girls' school in Lebanon, established alternative learning programs for out-of-school and married girls in Nigeria, and provided former female domestic laborers with education in Pakistan.

I DID INTERVIEWS FROM MY RED HONDA CIVIC AS MY BEST FRIEND DROVE ME TO LIVE NEWS INTERVIEWS.

After a few radio interviews I returned to school (trying not to skip a lot of classes—that would be too ironic). I was ecstatic to receive messages from people saying they would donate to the fund, and I assumed that was about as far as my story would spread. Then my cell phone rang during English class: it was someone calling from the CBC, the main broadcasting network in Canada. The following

MTV.COM

TEENVOGUE.COM

TODAY STYLE

CTV NEWS

KISS 103.1

BUZZFEED NEWS

DAILYMAIL.CO.UK

GLOBAL NEWS

COSMOPOLITAN.COM

THE GLOBE AND MAIL

HUFFINGTON POST

SEVENTEEN.COM

HELLOGIGGLES.COM

NYMAG.COM

three days were a complete blur. I did interviews from my red Honda Civic as my best friend, Emily, drove me to live news interviews. I emailed images to countries I'd never been to, and I received thousands of messages from people all around the world saying my story had affected them and they were going to donate. I spoke out about women's rights over the phone in the school bathroom, and heard people say that my story had encouraged them to reflect on their own lives.

AS YOU CAN TELL, I'M A BIT OF A MALALA FAN GIRL.

My newsfeed was full of links to *Teen Vogue* images of the dress and BuzzFeed articles on "the teen standing up for women's rights." Soon the Malala Fund contacted me directly, and I was honored to be asked to write an article on women's rights for Malala's website. When I emailed the article to the Fund, I couldn't help but ask *Will Malala ever read this?* When someone responded with *She always checks it :D*, I squealed. As you can tell, I'm a bit of a Malala fan girl.

Chaudhry Faisal Mushtaq, founder of the Roots National Institute of Teacher Training and Education, presents Malala with a scholarship for studies at Roots Millennium Schools worldwide. BITES85/WIKIPEDIA.COM

"Let us remember: One book, one pen, one child, and one teacher can change the world."

—*Malala Yousafzai*

Array Mohamed looks at her copy of *I am Malala* in Denver, Colorado, where Malala spoke about her life and inspired young girls.
BRENT LEWIS/GETTY IMAGES

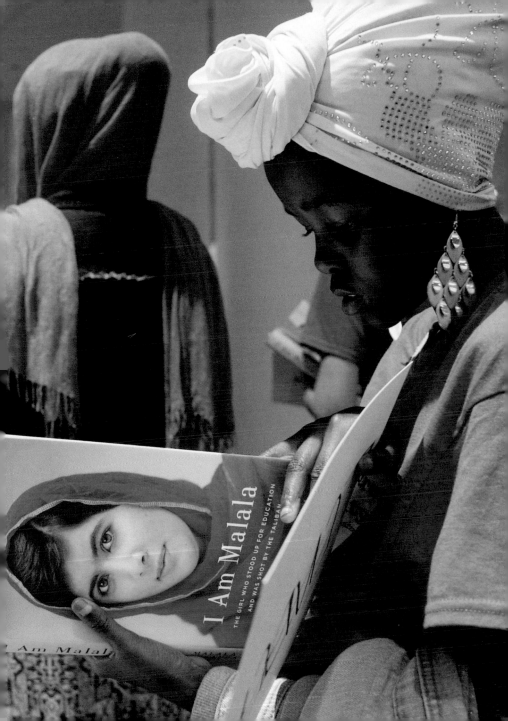

2

HOW SMART IS YOUR SMARTPHONE?

SO WHAT CAUSED THE STORY of my prom dress, which was worn for one evening in a small city on Canada's west coast, to reach from Romania to Thailand to London? To prompt an international conversation on women's rights and high school prom culture? The one common denominator was my smartphone.

At the time I had a blue iPhone 4, with a cracked screen (don't ask) and a malfunctioning Home button. None of that made any difference to the small device's ability to connect me to millions of people with a few taps and swipes.

FIRST STEPS

I had first gotten Facebook at thirteen (and yes, I actually waited until the legal age to sign up). My profile picture was of my dog, and I used it mostly to broadcast my comments on new *Glee* episodes. I first learned what *activism* was around this age as well. I attended an event called WE Day, which brings together pre-teens and teens from across the country who are interested in making a difference in their local and global communities. When I heard about the event, I asked my leadership teacher to take a group of us on the ferry to Vancouver to attend.

The day consisted of musical performances by Demi Lovato and the Barenaked Ladies, and inspirational speeches from international icons like Al Gore. With nearly 20,000 other students in attendance, this was the first time I also realized the power there is in numbers. You can't buy a ticket to attend WE Day; you must *volunteer* and earn the

"The change starts within each one of us. And ends only when all children are free to be children."

—*Craig Kielburger,
WE Day founder*

ticket through giving back to your local and global community. WE Day now takes place in fourteen different cities in three countries. It has helped raise over $62 million for more than 2,500 different local and global causes, and student attendees have tracked almost 20 million volunteer hours.

I had an interest in activism even before WE Day, but I didn't really know what *social justice* was. I couldn't wrap my head around the idea that others were suffering mainly due to the circumstances they were born into. I got to cuddle my dog, watch *George Shrinks* on TV and eat Cheezies while other kids couldn't access clean water, had no place to live or were working in forced labor for eighteen hours a day.

When I was in high school, I volunteered at care facilities for the elderly, collected warm clothes for the homeless and helped develop a *sustainable* community gardening initiative in my neighborhood. I loved the feeling of helping others, making a difference and influencing the world around me: I was hooked on activism and wanted more.

BY THE NUMBERS

1 According to the United States Department of Housing and Urban Development's 2014 Point-in-Time Report, **34 percent of the total homeless population in the United States is under the age of 24**. [dosomething.org]

2 **Poor nutrition causes nearly half (45 percent) of deaths in children under five**—3.1 million children each year worldwide. [wfp.org]

3 **Nearly 50 percent of people living in extreme poverty are 18 or under.** [stophungernow.org]

4 If present trends continue, over the next decade **150 million girls will be married before their 18th birthday**. That's an average of 15 million girls each year. [icrw.org]

5 In 2013, there were **16.7 million refugees** worldwide; an estimated **50 percent were under 18**. [dosomething.org]

From top left to right: Delegates begin to arrive at the first ever WE Day UK; Malala waves to the crowd; Prince Harry addresses the gathering; images of live performances are projected on screens.
ERINNE PAISLEY

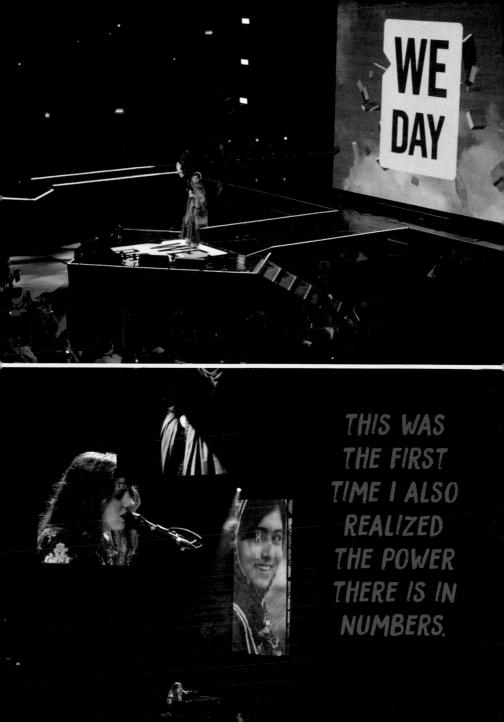

THIS WAS THE FIRST TIME I ALSO REALIZED THE POWER THERE IS IN NUMBERS.

ACTION NOW

I started to wonder what I could do to affect the lives of people outside my local community. In grade 10 I co-founded an activist group called Action Now with my friends Faelan and Griffin. Getting to work with two older students who were actually interested in what I had to say was pretty much the coolest thing that had ever happened to me. We all agreed that we wanted to make a difference in the world and take "action now" (hence the fairly self-explanatory name, which still took us more than two weeks to come up with and in the end was one of our moms' ideas). The three pillars of the group were: 1) learning 2) discussion 3) action. We led school-wide discussions on topics such as social justice and environmental protection. We constructed a positive blackboard initiative to promote mental health, and we hosted guest speakers such as Green Party of Canada leader and Member of Parliament Elizabeth May.

By the time I was in Grade 12, Action Now was growing in numbers, but Griffin and Faelan had both

I LOVED THE FEELING OF HELPING OTHERS, MAKING A DIFFERENCE AND INFLUENCING THE WORLD AROUND ME.

Me, Griffin Marsh and Faelan Prentice, co-founders of Action Now.
JULIA MENARD

graduated. We had always decided the topic for the year's activities together, but this time I was on my own. I turned to the rest of the group and together we brainstormed until we found something we were all passionate about: *social media*. The topic may have seemed unrelated to social justice, but we wanted to connect with others far beyond our high school walls, share our stories, hear from others, and open up discussions on important issues. Social media seemed the best way to accomplish that. And our smartphones were our best tools.

#COOLTOCARE

This was my first real personal experience with social media activism. We filmed and edited a YouTube video on women's rights called "#cooltocare". The video got a few hundred views, which in the grand scheme of YouTube views isn't really that much. But it was being shared with parents and friends who wouldn't have seen it otherwise, and we were pretty happy with ourselves. Using social media, we had opened up a discussion on gender equality.

In 2015 I took part in the Women in House program in Ottawa, ON. We shadowed Canadian female MPs for International Women's Day. From left to right: Me, Jessie Xie, Angela Hou and Alejandra Bellatin. MAYA HOKE

EFFECTIVE ACTIVISM ALWAYS STARTS WITH A CONVERSATION, WHICH IDEALLY LEADS TO QUESTIONING THE WAY THINGS ARE

The more I thought about it, the more sense it made to use the power of social media to make activism effective. When you're trying to make a difference, there is always more power in numbers. I had first learned this at thirteen, sitting in the WE Day crowd, awkwardly head-bobbing to Demi Lovato and chanting with thousands of others that we were "the leaders of today." Effective activism always starts with a conversation, which ideally leads to questioning the way things are and inquiring into whether there is the possibility of improvement. Using social media, this process can happen very quickly and on a large scale.

I had not thought a lot about the power of combining social media and activism until the story of my paper dress took on a life of its own. It started with social media and led to charitable

CREATE YOUR OWN AWARENESS

Action Now's YouTube video "#cooltocare" was an example of an *awareness campaign*. An awareness campaign is a project that tries to initiate a conversation on a specific topic and bring awareness to it. Prompting a conversation can shift people's mindsets. It's very easy to get stuck seeing a situation from one point of view, but when you have a conversation, it opens your mind to seeing things from various perspectives.

USING SOCIAL MEDIA, WE HAD OPENED UP A DISCUSSION ON GENDER EQUALITY.

POP QUIZ

With a group of friends, think of a topic that matters to you and brainstorm as many perspectives on that topic as you can.

How many can you come up with?

How can you encourage a bigger conversation on this topic in your community that would include even more perspectives?

Starting a conversation about a topic that matters is always the first step to making change happen.

actions without my direct involvement. More and more people were joining the conversation.

As a teenager with an iPhone, I often hear people talk about my generation's supposed laziness and rudeness. "You're always glued to your phone" is the modern-day equivalent of "You're always listening to that horrible rock music." I will admit that I never go anywhere without my phone, but what this small object can do goes far beyond exchanging texts or sharing funny cat videos. I belong to a generation connected by technology, a generation itching to make change, and a generation armed with cheesy usernames.

I BELONG TO A GENERATION CONNECTED BY TECHNOLOGY, A GENERATION ITCHING TO MAKE CHANGE, AND A GENERATION ARMED WITH CHEESY USERNAMES.

"The most important
equation to learn is
give + issue = change."

—*WE Day Toronto, 2014*

3

A BOY SCOUT, AN ARTIST AND A RAPPER

WHAT DO A BOY SCOUT, AN ARTIST and a rapper have in common? They have all used social media to help change our world. Sometimes it only takes one person to make a difference. Ryan, Rosea and Sofia were all teenagers when they decided that something in their world had to change and they were going to make it happen!

THE BOY SCOUT

In 2013, Ryan Andresen was in his last year of high school. He had already accomplished a lot: finishing high school, coming out to his friends and family as gay, and completing every step to earning his Boy Scout Eagle Award.

The Eagle Award is the highest ranking you can receive within the Boy Scouts of America and takes years of work to earn. Ryan had participated in Boy Scouts since he was six years old and had even created a *Tolerance Wall* in his school for his final Boy Scouts project. When he was about to earn his award, he was told he could not receive it because he had recently come out as gay.

His mom immediately used social media to ask others to help Ryan. She wrote and shared a *petition* on Change.org that anyone from around the world could sign. Many people could now hear Ryan's story and support him with just a few clicks.

The petition, which was called Overturn Ban on Gay Scouts, asked Ryan's local Scout Council executive to stop discriminating against LGBTQ members.

POP QUIZ

Over 100 million people have used the Change.org website and the number continues to grow.

Every single day new petitions are started.

What would you petition for if you were able to ask anyone in the world for support?

Start your own petition and view others on Change.org today.

Ryan and his mom wanted everybody to be accepted and allowed to be a part of the Boy Scouts of America community. People from all over the world signed the petition. Ellen DeGeneres saw Ryan's story and invited him on her TV show.

The Boy Scouts of America's National Council voted on the rule—and they reversed it! More than 479,000 people had signed the petition and shared it on Facebook, Twitter and other social media platforms.

This collage was created by a member of Scouts for Equality, a nonprofit organization that believes the Boy Scouts of America should fight against discrimination and for equality. BRIAN PEFFLY, SCOUTS FOR EQUALITY

POP QUIZ

Creating a Tumblr blog is completely free; all you need is an email address.

There are over 280 million different blogs on the website right now [as of February 20, 2016]!

What conversation would you choose to start on your blog?

THE ARTIST

Rosea Lake was in chemistry class, staring at the beakers, when she started thinking about how girls are judged based on what they wear. Some are called sluts for wearing too little, and others are called prudes for wearing too much. Every person should be equally free to wear what they want, without judgments from others. Rosea wanted to show this and discuss it more.

In art class, she decided to express herself using photography and a computer. She called the piece "Judgments." She got a B on the art project, and forgot all about it. A year later she decided to post it on her Tumblr, *RoseaPosey.tumblr.com*. Right away, people started re-blogging it. After only a couple of days, more than 280,000 people had shared it!

She started getting requests to give interviews on the piece, and spoke up about gender equality and expectations placed on girls and women. "I'm just happy that it has sparked so much dialogue and conversation. The message is much more important than I am, so I want people to use it," she said in

#MYCHOICENOTYOURS

WHORE
SLUT
ASKING FOR IT
PROVOCATIVE

CHEEKY

FLIRTY

PROPER

OLD FASHIONED

PRUDISH

MATRONLY

Rosea Lake with "Judgments."
ROSEA POMONA LAKE

"OUR SOCIETY IS READY TO TALK ABOUT [SLUT-SHAMING]. THIS JUST SORT OF GAVE IT A PUSH."

one interview. "Our society is ready to talk about [slut-shaming]. This just sort of gave it a push."

The image has been re-blogged over a million times and started an international conversation about equality. Rosea is studying graphic design and illustration at Capilano University in Vancouver, British Columbia, and is learning how to construct images that will encourage global conversations on important issues.

THE RAPPER

In July 2015, a YouTube video featuring the rapper Sofia Ashraf was released. This was no ordinary rap video. It was set to Nicki Minaj's song "Anaconda," but its new lyrics had lines like "Unilever came

Rosea's original art piece "Judgments" was created when she took a picture of her friend's leg and wrote labels on it. ROSEA POMONA LAKE

and left devastation, as they exposed the land to contamination" and "Kodaikanal won't step down until you make amends now."

Unilever is a massive *conglomerate* that owns companies like Dove, Lipton and even Ben & Jerry's ice cream. There used to be a Unilever factory in Kodaikanal, in southern India. The factory used mercury to make thermometers, and the mercury poisoned over a thousand workers who were not given proper protective gear. In 2001 the factory was shut down, but it had already hurt many people, and the surrounding environment was polluted. The mercury pollution is still hurting people in the area, even years later.

SOFIA'S MUSIC VIDEO WAS MADE TO BRING ATTENTION TO THIS ISSUE, AND SHE ASKED PEOPLE TO SIGN A PETITION ONLINE.

Sofia's music video was made to bring attention to this issue, and she asked people to sign a petition online demanding that Unilever "take responsibility for Kodaikanal

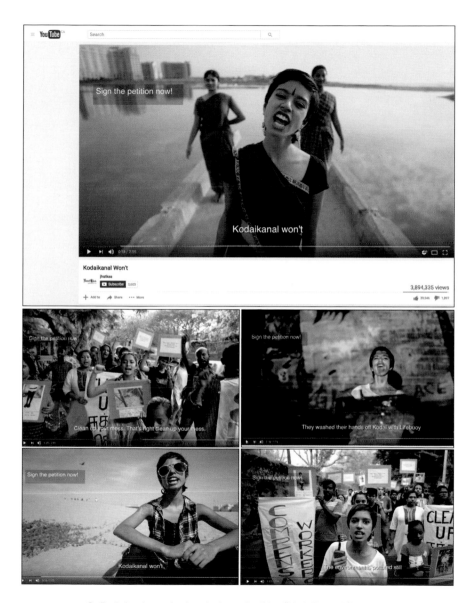

Sofia Ashraf raps in the viral music video "Kodaikanal Won't"
along with other activists. KODAIKANAL WON'T/YOUTUBE.COM

mercury poisoning." Once the video was posted, people all over the world started to share the message. Nicki Minaj saw the video and tweeted it to her more than 20 million followers. Now the video has had almost 4 million views!

Unilever's CEO tweeted a response to the video. Jayaraman, the activist group that Sofia worked with, had been trying to talk to Unilever about these issues since the factory was first closed in 2001. They had never had any response before. The CEO denied any responsibility for the poisonings, and the petition is still in place, helping to put pressure on a humongous company to modify its standards for how it treats both people and the environment.

How can you make a difference and start a meaningful conversation around the world like Ryan, Rosea and Sofia? All progress has to start somewhere, and that somewhere can be with you. Take a stand, use your creativity and help those around you. Everything starts by learning more, and one thing we've definitely learned so far is: what you click on can have a serious impact.

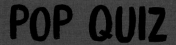

POP QUIZ

If you could talk to the bosses of any company and ask them to make a change, what would you ask for?

Online, you can find the contact information of company heads, often under the About or Contact tab.

Write a letter to a CEO today; you never know who might respond and what conversation you might be able to start.

In January 2017, women's marches were held all around the world in support of women's rights and equality. I took part in the Toronto march, which was nearly 60,000 strong! HEATHER NICHOLS

4

CAN YOUTUBE CHANGE THE WORLD?

YOUTUBE HAS BEEN AROUND SINCE 2005, and in that time it has grown to have more than a BILLION users. There are also billions of views every single day. Vloggers like Tyler Oakley and Zoella have become celebrities, and videos like "Cat Jump Fail" have gone completely viral.

YouTube is watched by a lot of people, and its power is huge. So what happens when this power is used for more than just views? When vlogs and videos are produced to advance our world?

STAMPING OUT STIGMA

Zoella's YouTube channel has over 11 million subscribers, and whether she's vlogging with Alfie, celebrating Christmas with ThatcherJoe or showing us a new haul, Zoe is always cheerful and ready to share. In 2012, Zoella filmed the video "Dealing with Panic Attacks & Anxiety," which let her viewers see a part of her life that she doesn't usually share. She showed us that if you have ever experienced anxiety, panic attacks or any other type of mental health challenge, you are not alone. She also gave tips about how to deal with panic attacks and anxiety: everything from drinking tea to listening to her favorite calm-down song.

Zoella has made more YouTube videos and blog posts about mental health since, and other people have posted YouTube video responses, sharing their own stories of dealing with anxiety. "We need to stamp out the stigma surrounding mental illness, and the first thing we need to do is talk about it more," Zoella says.

POP QUIZ

Zoella used a challenge in her life to support and help others who are challenged by it too.

What challenge in your life do you think others experience?

Start a conversation online about an issue that affects you by sharing your own story and creating solidarity with others who are experiencing the same thing.

How can you help them while also helping yourself?

You Tube 101

How can you make a YouTube video with a bigger purpose?

1. Give an overview of the issue you're focusing on, either by explaining it, showing it or creating a fictional story to illustrate it.

2. Suggest ways to address the issue, show ways to solve it or share how you are already helping.

3. Explain to the audience how they can join in and help too.

4. Make sure to clearly provide further links and resources for the audience to access. This could be a way to track the project's progress (on a Facebook page, for example), a way to ask more questions about the project, or a way for people to get involved immediately online. Get filming on your smartphone, laptop or camera today!

ALL THE SAME LOVE

When Macklemore and Ryan Lewis were about to drop their new music video for "Same Love," many fans were extremely excited. Would this be another "Thrift Shop"-style video or would it be a whole new thing? When the video came out, it was clear that Macklemore and Ryan Lewis's message was more serious than ever before. Lyrics like "underneath it's all the same love—damn right I support it" forced people to think about how unjust it was that same-sex marriage was still illegal in the United States.

"It's human rights for everyone, there is no difference. Live on, and be yourself," Macklemore raps in the video as a love story of two men plays out behind him. When Macklemore, Ryan Lewis and Mary Lambert performed "Same Love" at the Grammys in 2014, real couples got married on stage. Talk about music changing the world!

In June 2015, three years after the song's release, the United States Supreme Court officially ruled that same-sex marriage is a legal right throughout all of the USA.

"IT'S HUMAN RIGHTS FOR
EVERYONE, THERE IS
NO DIFFERENCE. LIVE ON,
AND BE YOURSELF."

—Macklemore

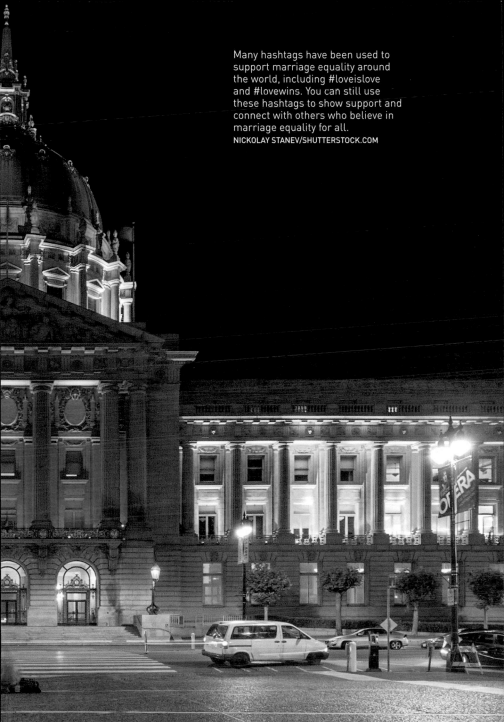

Many hashtags have been used to support marriage equality around the world, including #loveislove and #lovewins. You can still use these hashtags to show support and connect with others who believe in marriage equality for all.

NICKOLAY STANEV/SHUTTERSTOCK.COM

DEFINING YOURSELF

In 2006, Lizzie Velasquez was the subject of an eight-second-long YouTube video called "The World's Ugliest Woman." The comments in the video made fun of her appearance and called her cruel names, and some even told her to end her life. Lizzie has a rare syndrome that makes it impossible for her to gain weight. The video made fun of her appearance and was an example of cyber-bullying. Instead of responding by being angry or sad or blaming people, she spoke out in a video of her own.

She asked the world "How Do YOU Define Yourself?" in her TedX Austin Women talk, which was posted online. Lizzie told people to use any negativity in their own lives to make themselves better people. "Am I going to let those who called me a monster define me? No. I'm going to let my goals and success and accomplishments define me, not my outer appearance."

Lizzie now has her own YouTube channel, where she shares her life and has worked on anti-bullying, pro-kindness campaigns like I Am A Witness.

THE DIFFERENT SIDES TO BULLYING

The Bystander Revolution is an online movement and website that shares ways to defuse bullying. On the website you can find YouTube videos of celebrities, like author John Green and actor Lily Collins telling their own stories of being bullied or talking about what it's like "Being The New Kid." There are resources for both those experiencing bullying and those doing the bullying, because everyone has a perspective that is beneficial to explore.

From top to bottom: Jack and Finn Harries speak at VidCon in 2014. Since then they have both helped push for positive environmental change around the world. GAGE SKIDMORE/WIKIPEDIA.ORG, WWF's logo is a giant panda, one of the first animals the World Wildlife Fund worked to protect. FLYTOSKY11 /DREAMSTIME.COM, This iceberg in Disko Bay, Greenland, is melting rapidly due to global warming. Melting icebergs can lead to further environmental dangers, such as rising sea levels. VADIM PETRAKOV/SHUTTERSTOCK.COM

CAN SUBSCRIBERS SAVE THE ENVIRONMENT?

Maybe you have watched JacksGap ever since he posted "My First YouTube video!" Or maybe you started watching when he tried to convince viewers that his twin Finn was fake. Either way, you've probably seen Jack and Finn Harries' faces somewhere online along with their 4.2 million other subscribers.

In 2015, Jack and Finn chose to tell a story with the World Wildlife Fund. The WWF is one of the world's biggest environmental conservation organizations, and Jack and Finn wanted to support it. Their video, "Our Changing Climate," has had more than a million views. The boys traveled to Greenland, where they filmed the ice sheets and the surrounding sea ice that are melting due to climate change. They also went to London to take part in the People's Climate March, and they talked about the COP21 Conference on Climate Change, which was about to happen in Paris.

POP QUIZ

Earth Day, which is on April 22 every year, is a time to honor our earth and take action to protect it.

What can you and your school do to celebrate and take action on Earth Day?

Does your school recycle? In my high school we had numerous recycling stations to try to create zero waste.

Visit earthday.org to learn more ways to take action.

POWER TO (TYLER OAKLEY'S) PEOPLE

From his "How To: Be A Bad B*tch" life tutorial, to his ongoing love story with Darren Criss, to his annual Chicken Nugget Challenge, Tyler Oakley is unapologetically himself and proud of it. Over 8 million people love watching him and have subscribed to his YouTube channel.

In 2014, Tyler was turning twenty-five years old. He asked his viewers to donate to the Trevor Project instead of sending him cards or gifts. The Trevor Project provides crisis intervention and suicide prevention to LGBTQ youth. It has a crisis hotline that has answered more than 100,000 phone calls. "You are literally saving lives by donating," Tyler says.

"YOU ARE LITERALLY SAVING LIVES BY DONATING."

Tyler and his "people" raised more than half a million dollars during his twenty-fifth birthday month! For his twenty-sixth birthday, another half a million was raised.

WHO KNOWS? MAYBE ONE HUNDRED VIEWS WILL TURN INTO ONE THOUSAND AND THEN MAYBE EVEN ONE MILLION.

Tyler held live streams and used Prizeo (every donation earns the donor the chance to win a prize) to raise money. In 2015 the grand prize for donating was a trip to VidCon and a backstage pass to hang out with Tyler himself.

When you're first starting out on YouTube, it's easy to wonder why you should be creating videos when you don't have millions of subscribers. Any YouTuber will tell you that the first time your video gets a few hundred views, the feeling is beyond exciting. You know that your message has reached an audience that it wouldn't have otherwise. Who knows? Maybe one hundred views will turn into one thousand and then maybe even one million.

POP QUIZ

What conversations have you joined through YouTube?

Which ones will you continue to support and subscribe to?

What would you wish for on your birthday that would benefit others even more than you?

Instead of traditional gifts, what gift could also give back?

"I feel like everybody, whether you have one follower or a million followers, has an opportunity to either positively or negatively affect people."

—*Tyler Oakley*

5

CAN YOUR #INSTA CHANGE THE WORLD?

ON MALALA'S EIGHTEENTH BIRTHDAY she didn't ask for presents. Instead she asked people to post a selfie on Instagram with the hashtag #booksnotbullets. In the selfie you had to include your favorite book and a message about why education is more powerful than weapons. Malala met with world leaders during the campaign and asked them to give money to education instead of to the military because **"books are more powerful than bullets."** She told them that if the world stopped spending money on the military for eight days and put that money toward education instead, then every single child in the world could get twelve free years of schooling.

Along with their selfies, people wrote messages to world leaders such as *With an education, you don't have to be afraid of anyone* and *Every child deserves an education and to be inspired by books.* I posted a picture of myself with my favorite book, *Slumdog Millionaire.* I wrote on Instagram *#booksnotbullets because education is a human right. Equal opportunities to education worldwide is the key to positive global development.* Over 20,000 people raised their voices with the hashtag #booksnotbullets.

On her birthday, Malala traveled to Lebanon and opened a new school for more than 200 girls. The school is called Malala Yousafzai All-Girls School.

A SELFLESS SELFIE

Has anyone ever told you that a selfie can't possibly help our world? Well, War Child, an organization that helps children who are affected by war, definitely does not agree. It provides education and job training to children and their families in order to improve their day-to-day living standards. Through these initiatives, families can start to build a safer and more peaceful future.

In 2016, War Child asked for help bringing awareness to its cause and raising funds. If you posted a selfie wearing your favorite band T-shirt and used the hashtag #WearItForWarChild, you were entered to win tickets to one of War Child's fundraising concerts in London. All the money from these concerts, which featured artists like Florence + the Machine and Cold Play, went to War Child.

My #booksnotbullets selfie. My favorite book is *Slumdog Millionaire* by Vikas Swarup. ERINNE PAISLEY

"Social media are a catalyst for the advancement of everyone's rights. It's where we're reminded that we're all human and all equal. It's where people can find and fight for a cause, global or local, popular or specialized, even when there are hundreds of miles between them."

—*Queen Rania of Jordan*

NO TO DOLPHIN SLAUGHTER
NO TO DOLPHIN CAPTIVITY

If you care ....
care for the wild.com

care for the wild
INTERNATIONAL
www.careforthewild.com

Maisie Williams holds up a sign supporting Care for the Wild, an organization that fights for animal rights and conservation.
LEON NEAL/GETTY IMAGES

ONE DIRECTION'S DOLPHINS

Not only has actor Maisie Williams recently teamed up with War Child to participate in the #WearItForWarChild campaign, but an Instagram video she posted of Harry Styles in concert also initiated a ripple of actions. This single post was no normal concert video. Harry asked the crowd, "Does anyone like dolphins?" and when he got an enthusiastic response, he yelled, "Don't go to Sea World!" Maisie posted the video with the hashtag #dontgotoseaworld, which started trending worldwide.

Maisie is a star on *Game of Thrones* and also an ambassador for Ric O'Barry's Dolphin Project, which advocates for the safety and wellbeing of dolphins worldwide and raises awareness of animal abuse in places like Sea World. With this single post, Maisie brought attention to what was happening to the dolphins at Sea World and encouraged people not to go there. Public pressure was put on Sea World to modify how it treats dolphins, but unfortunately the abuse continues. You can visit dolphinproject.com to find out about ways that you can get involved in saving the dolphins.

#FOODSTAGRAM FEEDS THE HOMELESS

Have you ever leaned over your dinner plate to get the right angle for a *foodstagram*? If you have, you are definitely not the only one. There are over 16 million #foodstagram posts on Instagram alone. Most of us take for granted that we will always have food on our plates. Now, by taking a foodstagram and adding the hashtag #mealforameal, you can help others have food on their plates too.

SINCE 2004 THEY HAVE GIVEN MORE THAN 53 MILLION MEALS TO THOSE WHO NEED THEM.

Every single year, more than 1.3 billion tonnes (1.4 billion US tons) of perishable food is thrown away around the world. In Australia, OzHarvest turns edible food waste created by places like grocery stores, hotels and restaurants into meals for Australians who are going hungry. OzHarvest collects surplus food and donates it to charitable organizations. If you tag any of your food Instagrams with the extra hashtag #mealforameal,

Next time you take a photograph of food, share it with the hashtag #mealforameal to help give someone a real meal. JOSHUA RESNICK/SHUTTERSTOCK.COM

then Virgin Mobile donates to OzHarvest and turns your foodstagram into a real meal for someone in need. Just one dollar provides two meals! Since 2004 they have given more than 53 million meals to those who need them. So next time you Instagram that yummy scone and latte, make sure to tag #mealforameal to turn that #foodstagram into a meal for someone else.

LET YOUR CREATIVITY SHINE

Do you like to draw? @feministthoughtbubble loves doodling and posts these doodles on Instagram. All of them include strong female characters and quotes about female positivity. What image could you sketch that would bring awareness to an issue?

POP QUIZ

What type of community could your Instagram account shape for others to join and contribute to?

What hashtag could gather all these stories together?

You can now go to Instagram's Explore page to see what hashtags and images are trending today.

What are you going to share with the world on Instagram today?

How could it benefit those around you?

A NEW ONLINE COMMUNITY IS BORN

Raymond Braun, AKA @raymondbraun on Instagram, identifies as gay, but before he found his online LGBTQ community, he felt very alone. Nobody on television, in movies or in his town seemed to be going through the same things he was. When he shared his story on Instagram, he found others who were experiencing the same things, and he started to feel more confident in who he was.

His #VisibleMe campaign on Instagram is creating a new community and place for everyone to express who they truly are. Raymond works with other LGBTQ youth to share their stories through the hashtag. He has thousands of followers and a YouTube channel with over 21,000 subscribers. "VisibleMe encourages everyone to celebrate diversity and embrace what makes them different. We all have that spark within us," he says. The stories share

"WE ALL HAVE THAT SPARK WITHIN US."

what he describes as "the passion, diversity, resilience, and brilliance of the LGBTQ community."

#IAMMORETHAN BULLYING

Kylie Jenner has almost 74 million followers on Instagram and has built a massive community through this. When she started her #IAmMoreThan campaign in 2015, she asked all her followers to help her stop bullying. The #IAmMoreThan campaign shares the stories of people who have been bullied but have "become heroes in their own way by taking #bullying and turning it into something positive." Kylie shared with the world that she had been bullied her whole life and was inspired by those who have overcome adversity. She wanted her followers to also feel inspired to overcome adversity and to help others do the same.

Kylie started by sharing six different stories of people who had been bullied. One of these stories was from Renee DuShane, who was born with Pfeiffer syndrome, a genetic disorder where the bones in your face do not fuse to your jaw.

When Renee looked at Tumblr and saw other people posting selfies and feeling confident, she decided to post more pictures of herself and ignore the negative comments. She told Kylie, "I am more than my forehead."

After the first six posts, Kylie has continued to re-post #IAmMoreThan selfies, including one from @heyshalice, who has alopecia, a condition that causes hair loss. Instead of dwelling on the negative, she chooses to say, "I am more than just a girl who was looked at differently."

ANYTHING SHARED THROUGH INSTAGRAM HAS THE POTENTIAL TO CONTRIBUTE SOMETHING GREAT TO THE WORLD.

Now, nearly 20,000 other people have shared their own #IAmMoreThan pictures and shown that they are more than what anyone else might label them!

An average of 80 million images are shared on Instagram each day. Whether it be a photo series, a single hashtag, or even a meaningful GIF, anything shared through Instagram has the potential to contribute something great to the world.

In Canada, one day a year is designated Pink Shirt Day. On this day people come together to show support for those who have experienced, or are experiencing, bullying. **JACKIE PATTON**

"Smartphones and social media expand our universe. We can connect with others or collect information easier and faster than ever."

—*Daniel Goleman*

6

CAN YOUR TWEET CHANGE THE WORLD?

TWITTER IS THE HOME OF THE HASHTAG. Millions of tweets are sent every day. The moment you use any hashtag, your tweet gets grouped together with other posts that have used that hashtag. Popular hashtags can even start "trending" if enough people use them. With millions of tweets and hashtags being posted every day, there is some serious power available to favorably affect the world through Twitter.

On January 27 every year, one hashtag in Canada has extra superpowers: #BellLetsTalk. For this one day, when this hashtag is posted, Bell donates five cents to mental health initiatives. The company also donates for every text message sent, mobile and long-distance call made, and share of its Facebook page. The most action always comes from Twitter, and in 2015 the hashtag was trending as number one on Twitter worldwide! These tweets raised over $6 million—one hashtag at a time.

NOT ONLY DOES THE HASHTAG RAISE MONEY, BUT IT ALSO WORKS TO END THE STIGMA AROUND MENTAL ILLNESS

Since 2010, Bell has raised over $100 million for mental health initiatives in Canada, and a lot of this has been through #BellLetsTalk tweets. Not only does the hashtag raise money, but it also works to end the stigma around mental illness by creating a place for people to share stories about their own experiences with mental illness and their ideas for promoting good mental health. Celebrities like Olympic medalist Clara Hughes and astronaut Chris Hadfield have also worked with the #BellLetsTalk project.

EVERYONE CAN BE A FEMINIST!

Many people think of feminism as something that only women care about. But Elizabeth Plank, AKA @feministabulous, started the hashtag #AllMenCan to ask men to talk about what it means to be a male feminist.

Tweets like **#AllMenCan believe in equality for every single person** and **#AllMenCan treat everyone equally with respect** sent the message that everyone has a part to play in creating worldwide gender equality. The #AllMenCan hashtag added to the changing way we see gender equality and helped to show the world that men can also be feminists.

Men from all over the world took part in the #allmencan campaign by posing with messages for gender equality. Here my friend Jeromy Kixmoller-Gosley poses with his sign. ERINNE PAISLEY

My friend Julia Freya (left) and I pose in support of the University of Toronto Women and Gender Studies Student Union and intersectional feminism.

GENERATING ADDED PRESSURE

In Canada, many Aboriginal women have been murdered or have gone missing. The facts about violence toward First Nations, Inuit and Métis women and girls are very scary. A lot of activists have asked the government to help end this violence by taking more action to protect at-risk women and girls. One online campaign in particular, #AmINext, put pressure on the government and bring more international awareness to this issue.

The #AmINext campaign was started by Holly Jarrett, who asked Aboriginal women and their supporters to pose with signs that said #AmINext and then post the images online. Twitter started to fill with this hashtag, and Holly said, "I really think that if people understand all of these issues and we start talking about them, the general Canadian public is not going to let these issues go." People also started to post images with the #ImNotNext hashtag, saying that they refuse to be victims of this violence.

#CELEBRATIONS

Hashtags can be used to unite people in dark times, and they can also be used to celebrate when activism has led to advances. The #LoveWins hashtag was used when the Supreme Court ruled that same-sex marriage was legal in all US states. The hashtag encouraged acceptance of all types of love.

The rainbow flag represents inclusion and acceptance of all sexualities and genders. UNWEIT/DREAMSTIME.COM

On the day when the decision was made, Twitter even added a rainbow heart to the #LoveWins hashtag to show its support. In only six hours, over 6.2 million tweets were shared under the hashtag. The messages shared stories of love and support and included tweets from President Obama and Lady Gaga. Many people also used the hashtag to talk about how much more work still needs to be done to see marriage equality in every country.

RESPONDING TO HATERS

Sometimes it feels as if you can't do anything about frustrating, inappropriate or inaccurate things that are said online or in the media because you are not able to contact the commenter directly. But when Nobel Prize–winning scientist Tim Hunt made some offensive comments in 2015, a group of scientists quickly responded on Twitter. He had remarked publicly that "the trouble with girls [is that] three things happen when they are in the lab: you fall in love with them, they fall in love with you, and when you criticize them, they cry." These comments not only are untrue, but they also demean female scientists and discourage girls from choosing science as a career.

Instead of getting mad, many female scientists decided to point out how ridiculous his statements were. They started sharing pictures of themselves in the lab with the #DistractinglySexy hashtag. Some of the pictures were of female scientists in their work outfits (often in lab coats or hazmat suits). Other images showed female scientists from history and talked about how they were more focused on doing their jobs than falling in love (or crying). This hashtag not only drew attention to the fact that female scientists should be as respected as male scientists, but it was also one of the funniest activist hashtags ever. Next time you see something online that you want to respond to, you may not be able to talk to the person directly, but you can

INSTEAD OF GETTING MAD, MANY FEMALE SCIENTISTS DECIDED TO POINT OUT HOW RIDICULOUS HIS STATEMENTS WERE.

construct an online response that others can join in (especially if you add a hashtag)!

Whether it's joining in on a Twitter hashtag to bring awareness to an issue, creating your own hashtag to respond to an international issue, or even tweeting to raise money for a charity—a small tweet can definitely turn into a bigger noise when others join in.

Chelcy Brumlow, a research assistant at one of the world's leading cancer research hospitals, posted this photo of herself on Twitter (#distractinglysexy) in response to Tim Hunt's sexist comments. CHELCY E. BRUMLOW, M.S.

KEEPING UP WITH OUR WORLD

Other activist hashtags that have been used in response to international issues include the following:

#ICantBreathe speaks out against police violence toward African American youth in the USA.

#BringBackOurGirls raised awareness of the 276 girls abducted from their school in Nigeria and put pressure on the Nigerian government to find the girls and bring them home safely.

#BlackLivesMatter was created in response to systemic racism in North America.

What other hashtags can you think of that have arisen from international events and asked the world to take action?

Hashtags can connect you with new communities and show the world what causes you support. RAWPIXELIMAGES/ DREAMSTIME.COM

POP QUIZ

What question could you ask the world that would prompt a larger conversation?

What hashtag could connect those answers and start a movement?

Are you an ally to any activist movements?

Check out Amnesty International's "Urgent Action Network" page on the AI website to learn about activists who need your support today.

7

SOCIAL MEDIA CHAMPIONS

THERE ARE SOME PEOPLE who have absolutely owned making a difference through social media and use more than one type of platform to do it! Rowan Blanchard, Brandon Stanton and Miley Cyrus are three of these people. They use all different types of online spaces and even create new ones. By combining their passions and talents with their smartphones, they show us how to start a conversation and move the world forward.

ROWAN BLANCHARD TAKES ON GENDER EQUALITY

Rowan Blanchard is not your average fifteen-year-old. She is the star of the Disney Channel show *Girl Meets World* and has been named an "insta-activist" by Vice.com. Through her Instagram account she has supported many online activist campaigns, including Planned Parenthood. She has also used Instagram to show support for Emma Watson's #HeForShe campaign for international gender equality. Rowan even made a speech at the US National Committee for United Nations Women Annual Conference in 2015 and live-streamed it on Google to show it to the rest of the world; the speech is available on YouTube and has had almost 100,000 views.

Rowan has posted on Instagram about Amy Poehler's #AskHerMore campaign, which encourages media to ask female entertainers more empowering questions than "Who are you wearing?" She has used Instagram to show her support for the #BlackLivesMatter campaign for racial equality and for the #LoveWins hashtag. She is a transgender ally and she helped Chloe Cross's yearbook quote about ridiculous high school dress-code rules for girls go viral.

Even though Rowan usually uses Instagram to amplify her voice, she has also used Tumblr to originate content. On her Tumblr page, she has written essays on topics like intersectional feminism and got many people to join the conversation.

YOU DON'T NEED TO BE FAMOUS TO SPEAK OUT ON ROOKIE— ANYONE CAN!

Rowan is friends with (and often Instagrams with) Tavi Gevinson, who founded *Rookie*, another online space for people to voice their opinions and open up bigger conversations on important topics. You don't need to be famous to speak out on *Rookie*—anyone can! Other online spaces, like *Hello Giggles* (founded by Zooey Deschanel and two of her friends), also accept writing from anyone.

"There was a point maybe two or three years ago when everyone referred to social media as this thing for girls who were obsessed with taking pictures of themselves. It was ridiculed. But people are now realizing that it's an amazing tool for reaching a much broader audience. You can use it in a way that's beautiful to you."

—*Rowan Blanchard*

Rowan Blanchard at WE Day California 2016. Her speech from that event can be found on YouTube. KATHY HUTCHINS/SHUTTERSTOCK.COM

POP QUIZ

What story do you want to tell?

What conversation do you want to start?

Write an article today and submit to an online platform, because you never know who the story might reach! Most pages have a Submission button you click to get more instructions on how to submit, or you can go to the About section to find contact information for more people who are a part of the organization.

BRANDON STANTON AND HUMANS OF NEW YORK

Brandon Stanton started his online photo blog, *Humans of New York*, to tell the stories of ordinary people who live in New York. He wanted to show that, underneath many of our differences, we are all simply human. The blog began on Tumblr, and most people found out about it on Facebook. Now it has almost 18 million likes on Facebook and 8 million followers on Instagram. Brandon used social media to share his passion with the world and to hatch a new way for other people's stories to be told.

Humans of New York has been used to help with numerous causes around the world. In 2015, Brandon traveled to Pakistan and met with activist Syeda Ghulam Fatima, who works through the NGO (*non-governmental organization*) Bonded Labor Liberation Front to stop modern slavery. After sharing Syeda's story with the world, Brandon also set up an Indiegogo online page so anyone could donate to her cause. Over $2.5 million has been raised to help Syeda's fight to end slavery.

Humans of New York has also helped raise money for the Mott Hall Bridges Academy in New York. It started when Brandon shared a picture of a boy named Vidal. Brandon asked him who inspired him the most, and Vidal responded, "My principal, Ms. Lopez." Vidal talked about how Ms. Lopez treats him and his fellow students with respect, and how this inspires them. The neighborhood that Vidal's school is in has the highest crime rate in New York City, and it is very hard to grow up there. After Brandon shared this story, many people wanted to help and eventually a scholarship program was started through donations.

Brandon's blog has raised over $700,000 for Syrian refugees in just three days. Through sharing other people's stories, Brandon was able to effect constructive development all over the world!

VIDAL TALKED ABOUT HOW MS. LOPEZ TREATS HIM AND HIS FELLOW STUDENTS WITH RESPECT, AND HOW THIS INSPIRES THEM.

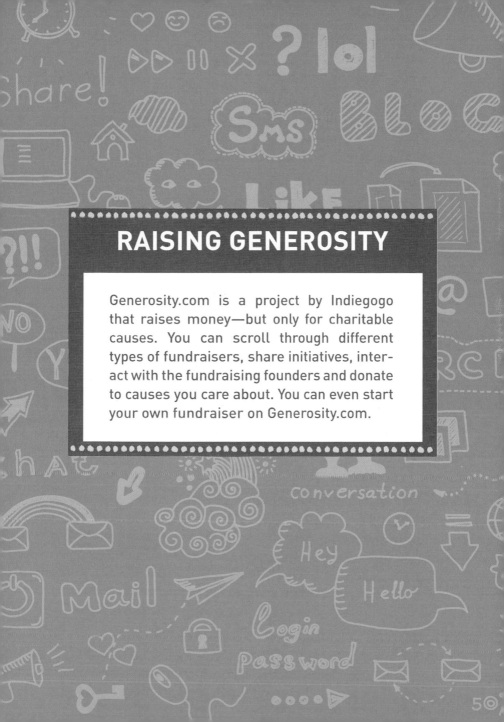

RAISING GENEROSITY

Generosity.com is a project by Indiegogo that raises money—but only for charitable causes. You can scroll through different types of fundraisers, share initiatives, interact with the fundraising founders and donate to causes you care about. You can even start your own fundraiser on Generosity.com.

MILEY CYRUS AND THE HAPPY HIPPIE FOUNDATION

Miley Cyrus has come a long way since she was Hannah Montana. She's produced a lot of new music, but she's also used social media to inspire progressive actions around the world. Miley constructed Backyard Sessions with Facebook to bring attention to her NGO, the Happy Hippie Foundation. Backyard Sessions was a series of musical jam sessions in her backyard with other celebrities like Ariana Grande. They were first broadcast on Facebook and then put on Miley's YouTube channel to bring both awareness and donations to the Happy Hippie Foundation, whose mission is to fight injustice faced by homeless youth, LGBTQ youth and other vulnerable populations. Miley's foundation works with many other organizations and charities to achieve this.

The Happy Hippie Foundation has over half a million followers on Instagram and has worked with Instagram on a campaign to bring awareness to these issues and its work. The #InstaPride campaign featured and celebrated transgender and gender-expansive individuals through a series of

PACIFICWILD

Miley Cyrus shows her support for Pacific Wild, an environmental nonprofit located in the Great Bear Rainforest in BC. IAN MCALLISTER

portraits. @jordvnhaus's portrait was featured on Instagram's official account, and he now has more than half a million followers on Instagram alone. He vlogged about the experience of meeting and working with Miley on his YouTube channel.

The Happy Hippie Foundation has also used Instagram to formulate encouraging messages. The Foundation asked all #happyhippies to post a #HappyHippieGram for LGBTQ youth in Los Angeles on Instagram, and then printed out some of the messages of love. These messages were then delivered to the Los Angeles LGBT Center.

Tumblr allows anyone to anonymously submit their stories of coming out, transitioning and questioning, which are then shared with the world. Messages of support can also be sent the same way.

Miley has supported many other activist movements through social media, like the environmental campaign to save BC wolves. The initiative was established by an activist group called Pacific Wild. Miley posted on Instagram about Pacific Wild's campaign to stop trophy hunting in British Columbia and shared images of herself in the Great

Bear Rainforest on the central coast of BC, where she was learning more about environmental issues. She encouraged everyone to post about #savebcwolves to bring awareness to the issues, donate to the cause and pressure the BC government to end the wolf kill.

Whether you choose to focus on one issue area or several, it's clear that combining more than one social media platform can lead to an even bigger impact. Which social media accounts do you use now? Try to use all of these resources to make an even greater difference.

Miley Cyrus poses with other young activists who are fighting to save BC wolves and preserve the province's wilderness. IAN MCALLISTER

POP QUIZ

Whose stories can you share with the world?

Who can you work with to foster developments?

How can you use social media to promote events or campaigns you are working on?

"The moment you stand up for something you believe in you are inviting others to join you—and you never know what type of ripple effect that can create!"

—*Erinne Paisley*

On November 28, 2016, I posted a video of myself on Instagram and Facebook in which I phoned a United States governor and requested that they stop attacks on protesters at Standing Rock and help stop the building of the Dakota Access Pipeline. I encouraged others to phone and tweet using the hashtags #nodapl, #standingrock and #standwithstandingrock.

popactivism
see change, about change, be change

8

ACTION NOW!

HERE ARE SOME THINGS YOU CAN DO with social media to make a differencc today!

FUNDRAISE

Bake sales can be very effective, but imagine how much more effective they could be if your #bakesale was trending online. Next time you are organizing a fundraising event at your school or in your community, start using social media to promote it. Design an online poster and add a hashtag to it. Get all your family and friends to use the hashtag when posting about the event. Set up a poster with the hashtag on it at the event and get people to take selfies with it to post online.

If you are fundraising for a cause, start talking to local businesses and ask them if they would commit to donating a certain amount in exchange for increased online attention. Would they donate 10 cents for every new like on their Facebook page for one day? Would they donate 25 cents for every direct tweet at them with a specific fundraising hashtag? Businesses benefit from increased online presence, and you can use your social media skills to turn those likes into actions. Mutually promote each other online to get more attention for both your cause and their business.

YOU CAN USE YOUR SOCIAL MEDIA SKILLS TO TURN THOSE LIKES INTO ACTIONS

There are multiple online sites that allow you to have people donate to your cause—even in exchange for prizes. You can use Prizeo, like Tyler Oakley does, to reward donors for giving specific amounts to your cause or to auction off something to raise funds. You could also have a fundraising goal online and get donors to help you reach your goal before a certain date—the fundraising countdown is on!

ADD YOUR VOICE

The old saying "there is strength in numbers" has stuck around for a reason—it's so true. You can easily add your voice and your support to online campaigns by using their hashtags. Tweet the campaign's hashtag or (if they have an account) tag them. On Instagram, you can also use a hashtag to join a campaign or even construct your own image of support. In 2015 there was a federal election in Canada, and many people were trying to encourage a better youth voter turnout. I cut out letters and designed my own Instagram image of support for the movement and even added the website link for how to vote. Use your creative skills to come up with a new way to show the world a pre-existing campaign.

"Social media is changing
the way we communicate
and the way we are perceived,
both positively and negatively.
Every time you post a photo
or update your status, you are
contributing to your own digital
footprint and personal brand."

—*Amy Jo Martin*

Amy Jo Martin, bestselling author and founder and
CEO of Digital Royalty. WORLD DOMINATION SUMMIT 2016

You can also use your social media accounts to create a new type of space to amplify campaigns. Use your iPhone to make a YouTube video telling the story of an activist campaign and put the links in the description so your viewers can contribute to the movement. If you own a Mac, iMovie is a way to edit movies for free on your computer. If not, you can download other editing software or take your video in just one shot. Anyone can upload to YouTube, and you can promote your video through other social media apps.

WE365

The creators of WE Day have now made their own app that helps you make a difference 365 days of the year. You can download it from the App Store for your smartphone. On it, accept challenges to make the world a better place every day or invent your own. You can also track your positive impact, be inspired by others, share and connect through the We365 community.

START YOUR OWN MOVEMENT

Do you have a passion to make a difference in your own way? If you do, it means that it's time to start your own social media activist project! The best thing about social media is that it is so new—every day more ways to start a movement online are being discovered and constructed. Remember to think outside the box. Look to other successful social media campaigns, start practicing using social media for activism and explore what is possible.

If you have a specific goal, a good way to start is with an online petition. Change.org allows you to set up a petition for anyone to sign. This petition can be a letter to a person, company, organization or government official. It can ask the recipient to stop doing a specific thing or to take a new action to shape a better world. The more people who sign it, the more likely it is that the recipient will be influenced by it and you will be able to reach your goal.

If you want to bring new attention to an important issue, think about what people are already paying

"Mental Illness is not a weakness, and the more we talk about it, the more we can support one another!"

—*Erinne Paisley*

Twenty percent of Canadians experience mental illness, and many more go undiagnosed or recorded. In July 2016, my friend Monique Sekhon wanted to help de-stigmatize mental illness and share mental-health resources with our community. She organized a #care2share event in Victoria, BC. Monique Sekhon (left) and me. MONIQUE SEKHON

attention to online and then add to that. For instance, you could make a YouTube parody of a trending music video the way Sofia did with her Unilever video. If the song is already trending, people who are searching for it online will also find your video.

Your words are more powerful than you know. If you have a story to share with the world, write it down, submit it to an online blog and start an important conversation with the world. When I wrote the article for Malala's blog, I never knew how many people it was going to reach or how big a conversation it was going to start. You can post your thoughts on your own social media sites, then use your sites to tell others' stories (always with their permission). Talk about amplifying voices online!

DO SOMETHING!

DoSomething.org is a website and movement designed to make it easier to have an impact on our world. You can find online campaigns on everything from posting positivity online to combating cyberbullying to saving hedgehogs. More than 5.3

With DoSomething, you can create a five-minute playlist to remind friends to take shorter showers. When the songs stop, the water goes off!
DO SOMETHING INC.

DoSomething works (and plays!) hard for important causes. The organization turned its office party into a fundraiser for orgs supporting the LGBTQ community.
DO SOMETHING INC.

You can take action on serious issues...but you don't always have to be serious while doing it. Just take it from the DoSomething staff!
DO SOMETHING INC.

million young people from over 131 countries are members of DoSomething.org and you can join them online.

CONTINUE TO CONNECT

One new place that you can share your activism story, and start an important conversation, is on my blog, PopActivism.com. I constructed this new platform to share stories about activism through social media. I get to write about activism in pop culture and share

SEE CHANGE,

SHARE CHANGE,

BE CHANGE

other people's activism projects. I can now further amplify my voice, and the voices of others, online. I also have Facebook and Twitter pages for the blog and promote it on all of my social media accounts.

More and more ways to use social media for activism are being created all the time—by people just like you! Each and every day new apps and hashtags are being invented or turned into resources for positive change. This book focuses largely on using YouTube, Instagram and Twitter, but these are just a few of the resources available to help you create change. Snapchat, Facebook, Pinterest, Vine and even Pokemon GO can be platforms for making a difference too. As our world continues to evolve, both online and offline, use what you have learned from reading *Can Your Smartphone Change the World?* as a jumping-off point for thinking about new ways to change our world.

Remember: see change, share change, be change. And don't forget to send me a tweet @popactivism so I can re-tweet it!

Supporting other people's endeavors is often just as important as starting your own. The more you connect with like-minded people, the more change you can make! Here I am with friends from the University of Toronto. GABBI LEON

Clockwise from top left: Handing out warm socks and lunches to the homeless in Victoria, BC; collecting shoebox hampers for those in need at Christmastime; presenting a fundraising check to the Canadian Cancer Society; leading a protest about students' educational rights in BC; rallying during the British Columbia Teachers' Federation's dispute; shaving my head for Cops for Cancer. ERINNE PAISLEY

Clockwise from top: With student Jessie Xie, MP Sheila Malcolmson and Renée Taylor on Parliament Hill in Ottawa, ON; at the Supreme Court of Canada in Ottawa; speaking at the Women in House program through the University of Toronto; meeting Prime Minister Justin Trudeau. **ALEJANDRA BELLATIN**

ADDITIONAL PHOTO CREDITS

GLOSSARY

activism—the creation of social and/or political change

awareness campaign—a project that tries to initiate a conversation on a specific topic and bring awareness to it

conglomerate—the combination of two or more corporations engaged in entirely different businesses that fall under one corporate group, usually involving a parent company and many subsidiaries; conglomerates are often large and multinational

foodstagram—a snapshot of a food moment posted on Instagram

LGBTQ—stands for lesbian, gay, bisexual, transgender and queer

NGO (non-governmental organization)—a not-for-profit organization that is independent from states and international governmental organizations

petition—a formal written request, typically one signed by many people, appealing to authority with respect to a particular cause

social justice—the way in which human rights are manifested in the everyday lives of people at every level of society

social media—online tools that allow people, companies and other organizations to create, share or exchange information, ideas and pictures/videos in virtual communities and networks

sustainable—able to be used without being completely used up or destroyed

volunteer—a person who freely offers to take part in an enterprise or undertake a task without getting paid

popactivism

see change. share change. be change.

RESOURCES

CHAPTER 1
www.malala.org

CHAPTER 2
www.weday.com

CHAPTER 3
www.change.org

CHAPTER 4
www.wwf.ca
www.mind.org.uk
www.prizeo.com
www.thetrevorproject.org
www.bystanderrevolution.org
www.earthday.ca

CHAPTER 5
www.warchild.org
www.ozharvest.org
www.dolphinproject.net

CHAPTER 6
letstalk.bell.ca
www.amnesty.ca

CHAPTER 7
www.humansofnewyork.com
www.generosity.com
www.happyhippies.org
www.pacificwild.org

CHAPTER 8
www.we365.com
www.dosomething.org
www.popactivism.com
www.erinnepaisley.com

ACKNOWLEDGMENTS

FIRST AND FOREMOST, I WOULD LIKE TO THANK Malala Yousafzai for not only inspiring me but also inspiring the world with her commitment to girls' education. Thank you to my mother and father for encouraging me to always create and explore. Thank you to my brother, Stuart Paisley, and Emily Faris for always being by my side.

I have been extremely fortunate to have a number of strong women in my life who have guided, inspired and believed in me. To name a few: Ti Hallas, Josie Bissonnette, the Rolands, Erin Hayes, Alana Charlton, Sara Reside, Angela Aarts, Heather Coey, Penny Barner, Susan Runholt, Member of Parliament Elizabeth May, and Professor Joy Fitzgibbon.

I also want to acknowledge Faelan Prentice, Griffin Marsh, Monique Sekhon, and all the others from Reynolds Secondary School who humored my crazy ideas and inspired me with their own. To my friends and mentors at Trinity College, University of Toronto, thank you for inspiring me every day, for being my second family, and for bringing iced caramel macchiatos to me at the library when I pulled all-nighters working on this project.

Almost all of *Can Your Smartphone Change the World?* was written during my first year at the University of Toronto, so I must also extend sincere gratitude to the St. Clair Balfour family and University of Toronto National Scholarship Program for giving me both the opportunity to attend U of T and the financial freedom to focus on this book.

Thank you to Ben Rudolph for designing the PopActivism logo. Thank you to Orca Book Publishers for believing in this project and helping it become a reality. Amy Collins, thank you for helping this project in its beginning stages. Sarah Harvey, thank you for believing in me since *Salieri's Diary* and making this book into more than I could have ever imagined.

Lastly, thank you to everyone who shared the story of my paper dress. I hope this book inspires you and helps you continue to create change.

ERINNE PAISLEY is an activist, public speaker, writer and student who made international headlines when she turned her math homework into a dress and wore it to her prom, then donated the money she would have spent on a dress to the Malala Fund. Now she is studying Peace, Conflict and Justice, as well as Book and Media Studies, at the University of Toronto. Erinne recently completed an internship at She's the First, an organization that provides scholarships, mentorship and empowerment to girls in low-income countries. She is the founder of PopActivism, a website devoted to promoting positive activism in pop culture.

Can Your Smartphone Change the World? is her first book. For more information, visit www.popactivism.com, or follow Erinne on social media.

- @popactivism
- @pop_activism
- Erinne Paisley

LOOK FOR THE NEXT TWO BOOKS IN THE

POPACTIVISM

SERIES

COMING SPRING 2018

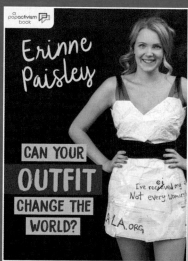

9781459813069 • PB • $14.95

COMING FALL 2018

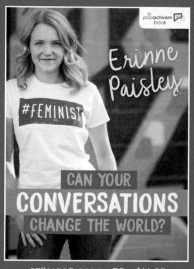

9781459813090 • PB • $14.95

ORCA BOOK PUBLISHERS
www.orcabook.com • 1-800-210-5277